Sisyphus and I

Ilja Kostovski

Translated by Donald Hitchcock

and Jack Hirschman

Washington, DC

Plamen Press

9039 Sligo Creek Pkwy, Suite 1114, Silver Spring, Maryland 20901

www. plamenpress.com

Published by Plamen Press, 2020

Printed in the United States of America

10 9 8 7 6 5 4 3 2 1

LIBRARY OF CONGRESS CATALOGING-IN-PUBLICATION DATA

Kostovski, Ilja

Sisyphus and I: Poetry Collection/Ilja Kostovski

p. cm.

ISBN: 978-0-9960722-4-3

Library of Congress Control Number:

218964425

Translated from the Macedonian by Donald Hitchcock

and Jack Hirschman

Cover Art by Igor Angelov

Cover Design by Roman Kostovski

Interior Art by Jarmila Kostovska

Editors

Rachel Miranda Feingold

Roman Kostovski

"The poems of Ilja Kostovski bring to bear —on a particular American moment—a voice that is both eternal and mythic in its scope. This body of work is at once caustic and holy, presenting readers with the incongruity and discomfort of a prophet who speaks to our own noisy, vulgar, and confusing political time. Alongside Ginsberg and Whitman, Kostovski joins a group of poets who have addressed America with tenderness, but also with the tense attention of a warning for what it is we might become."

—Mark Wunderlich, American poet, Lambda Literary Award winner; director, Bennington Writing Seminars

"What a marvelous soul was Ilja Kostovski, a poet possesed by all the gods and nature, he had a poetic enthusiasm that was irresistible and I am pleased to be part of his translation team. He was at home with the gods like a narodnik, and yet he lived his life as a true contempary of the Soviet years."

—Jack Hirschman, American poet, author of All That's Left
Emeritus Poet Laureate of San Francisco

"The poems of Ilja Kostovski, so Macedonian, and so American at the same time, are the meta-physical mirror of our own lives. His words reflect true post-religious, political poetry for a post-God, political time, showing us in an honest and powerful way that only love can save the world and all of us *losers* in it."

—Lidija Dimkovska, Macedonian Poet, author of A Spare Life
Winner of the 2013 European Union Prize for Literature

"Why was man created? One ponders this question while reading the poetry of Ilja Kostovski. His voice echoes those of prophets crying in the wilderness. Faith is often tested by the weight of the cross. How do we live without pain? The words of Kostovski breathe magic back into our air. His voice at times sounds like Whitman. In *Sisyphus and I* - I hear a poet's soul singing. Is it possible for Sisyphus to survive the heavy blues?"

—E. Ethelbert Miller, American poet, literary activist, editor of Poet Lore *magazine; author of* Fathering Words

"*Sisyphus and I* reads at once like ancient songs and intimate conversations. This writing overflows with the passions of a poet who saw much and felt deeply...Kostovski cries to heaven and to you and me like a modern psalmist—singing songs of worry and joy about a baffling, disjointed world."

—Elijah Burrell, American poet, author of Troubler *and* The Skin of the River

'Ilja Kostovski is an angry man. He rages at God and religion, at poverty and injustice, at the sort of poets whose faces "resemble lobsters and steaks." He venerates Abraham Lincoln, the toothless and the drunk, those who break windows and throw stones. Like Jack Gilbert, he's conversant in mythic landscapes and Greek gods. Befriended by Lawrence Ferlinghetti and Jack Hirschman (who's also one of his translators), Kostovski creates the world in his own image, singing of himself like Whitman and Mayakovsky. Multilingual bard, teacher, philosopher, wanderer, medieval rat catcher, stuntman: Ilja Kostovski is a force of nature. This collection is stunning in every sense of the word.

— Katherine E. Yonng, American poet, author of Day of the Border Guards
Inagural Poet Laureate of Arlington, Va

Table of Contents

FOREWORD

Ilja Kostovski: The Global Phenomenon with a Macedonian Soul

Jordan Plevnes

Translated from the Macedonian by Roman Kostovski

IIja Kostovski (1933-2017) was a true anti-Babylonian poet, who in the realm of his creative horizon had the ability to lift his voice in all the 6346 languages spoken on this planet Earth and yet, at the same time, to merge his verses into one unique and timeless tongue.

I met Ilja for the first time just after *The New York Times* published an article about the US-French production of my play, *Happiness is a New Idea in Europe*. It was in the medieval palace of Kursumli An in Skopje, the capital of Macedonia. He was reading one of his most famous verses, which I have quoted to many thirsty wordmongers all over the world:

In the Black Churches of Saint Louis
A last kiss hanged itself last night

I wrote about my friend during my literary youth in the oldest existing Macedonian newspaper, *Nova Makedonija*: "He is a poet who has learned all the languages of the world but was banned from speaking his own mother tongue." Our friendship has crossed over several decades, two centuries, and two millennia.

When you read the poetry of Ilja Kostovski, you cannot help but feel that he was an ancient poet like those of the rhapsodies recited in the era of great epics long sprung somewhere between the Balkans and Asia.

When you read the poetry of Ilja Kostovski, you cannot help but feel that the words of Aeschylus—"We are just fragments from the great banquet of Homer"—appear before our eyes and hearts, and suddenly we can't tell whether we've been hit by the waves of the Aegean shore in Kostovski's birthplace; or we've just landed in a library stacked with the entire collection of Europe's poetic memories; or we are traveling with him to the New World, and all the ancient scrolls of poetry are scattered among the meridians.

When you read the poetry of Ilja Kostovski, you can't help but feel that within a single hour, 3000 years suddenly passed, and you don't know where you are because he takes you among the 30,000 refugees counted by Herodotus during the Greco-Persian wars, and at the same time among the modern-day refugees migrating in directions unknown, that according to the UN have reached over 273 million.

When you read the poetry of Ilja Kostovski, you ask fundamental questions of civilization: What did God do before He created the Earth? From the brick and mortar of his life, Ilja Kostovski erected an unprecedented temple of words that sheltered all the languages he studied and spoke, and his verses resemble those minuscule churches of his native Macedonia with their tiny medieval angels, where a European renaissance was born amidst structures that housed all the religions of the world.

And this is what makes Ilja Kostovski a global phenomenon with a Macedonian soul. This soul is engraved in the encyclopedia of Kostovski's heart. It is found in the letters between Vincent Van Gogh and his brother, Theo, where the famous painter of *Sunflowers* once wrote: "And a vision appeared to Paul in the night; There stood a man of Macedonia who told us that without love we have nothing."

What good is a Hallelujah without sweet kisses?

Even today, in the modern and post-modern world of literary expression, love remains central to the world, irrespective of whether you write in Washington DC, Moscow, Beijing, Berlin, or Tokyo—or in a lost village somewhere in the Andes Mountains of Latin America.

I would meet up randomly with Ilja Kostovski in various cities throughout Europe and the world. One time, we were at an ancient poetry festival, the Struga Poetry Evenings, where he had once defiantly proclaimed: "Poetry's arsenal of words will always be more powerful than all the nuclear weapons aimed to destroy human hope."

When you read the poetry of Ilja Kostovski, you understand that the history of Sisyphus is the history of each individual—and at the same time, of the collective world. You understand that the individual cross you bear is transformed into a different burden when the destiny of one is cast into the destiny of millions.

That is why Ilja Kostovski was a global phenomenon of the Macedonian soul and of universal love, because Macedonia and the universe have one thing in common: they share the same border.

May 1, 2018—Paris

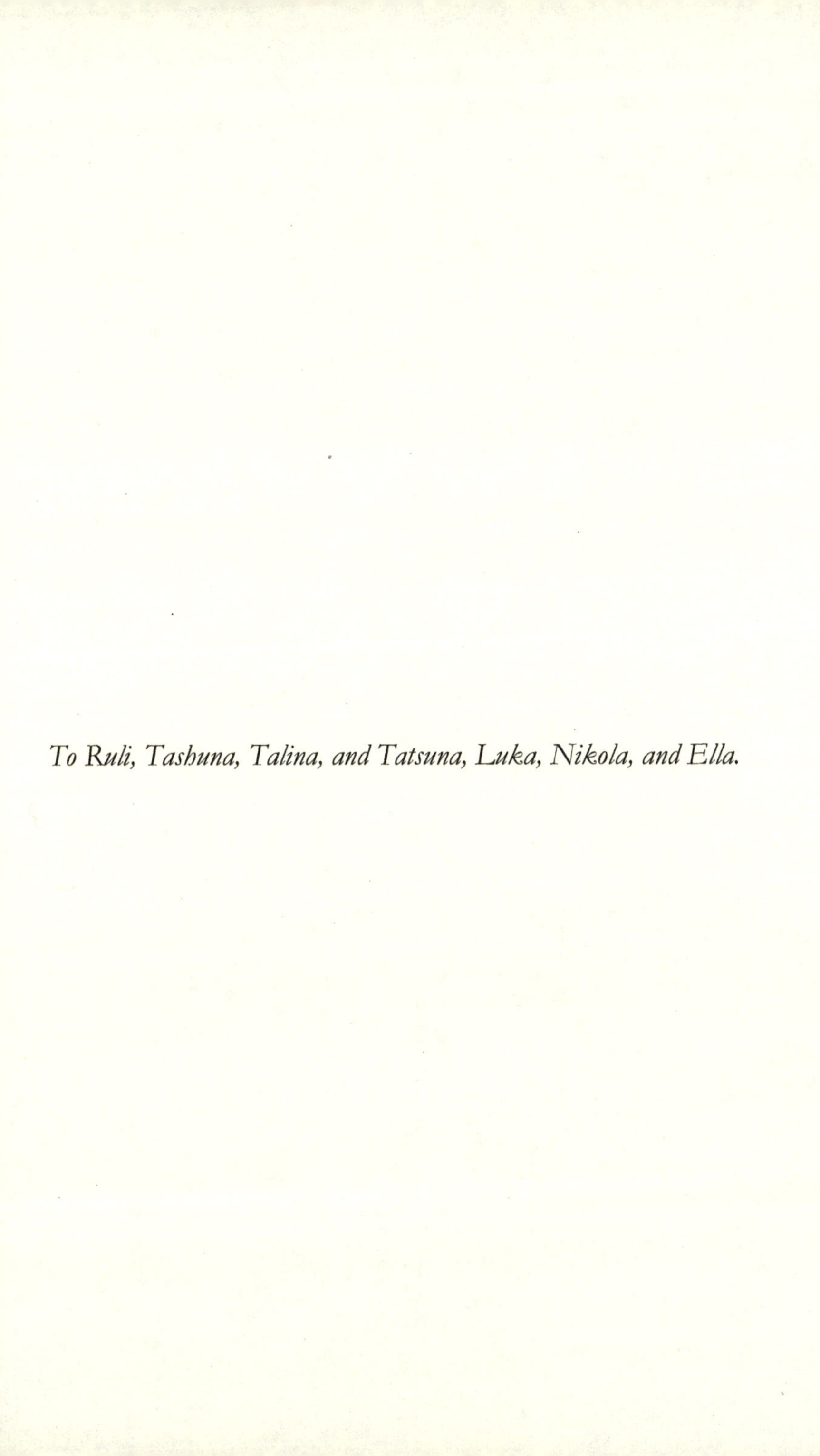

To Ruli, Tashuna, Talina, and Tatsuna, Luka, Nikola, and Ella.

Sisyphus and I

Ilja Kostovski

Talks with God

Translated by Donald Hitchcock

They say, God, you made the earth
The earth was invisible and desolate
And your spirit moved upon the earth
There was dry land and water
There was night
There was day
The skies were bright
There was heat, there were snows

In the harmonious game of elements
You found the icon of your mind
In your conception of the earth
The fish, fowl, and flocks
Were fruitful after their kind
The trees passionately multiplied
On the mountains and the hills

And you saw
That it was good and beautiful
Why did you need me?
Why did you throw a flaming torch
Into your ripe wheat fields?
I know the earth could easily exist
Without man, without me

Like a lamb without a wild beast
Like a dove without a falcon or eagle
Without hate, without greed
Without the knowledge of good and evil
The plentiful earth
Without saddle, bridle, and spurs
The earth free
Like a wild horse

But I know
You were the only one, my Lord
Who could not be on Earth
Without my word.

You needed me
To admire you.
Without me
Your hearth was cold
Without me
Your house had no fire
And you said
"Let us make man
In Our image,
After Our likeness."
And you created me…
Wait, God.
Did you carve my head
In the image of yours?
My wavy hair
My eagle nose

When you were walking
Along the Milky Way
What sound did you gather
To compose my resonant voice?
Did you take the orange glow
Of the sunset oceans
To create the color of my speech?
Behold me!
I will open my mouth.
Mount Sinai
Will shine from my words
As it did from yours.

Why since that time
Have you thundered
"I am the Lord
And you, my servant"?
Did you mold my pain
After your pain?
My eyes and my torments
After your own?
The dew of my lips
The sweep of my steps
My anguish, my hands
In the likeness of yours?

The beat of my heart
After the beat of yours
My inescapable love
In the image of yours?

Tell me, Lord
Up in the sky
What sap or juice
Did you choose
For my rebellious blood?

One day, God
Only once did you take
Clay and create me.
And how many times
Have I created you?
From granite
Multicolored flint
From horizon to horizon
Have I painted you in the clouds
In the stormy wind
Have I formed you from silver and gold.
To you, only, did I dedicate
My orchards and my groves
The first juice of my soil
The first fruit of my labor.
And my ploughed lands
Did I present to you
With my shaking hands.
In the canyons have I burned limestone
For the whiteness of your bell-towers.

Like the Sword of Damocles
Your will hangs over me
And your tablets of stone

When I was molding you
From clay on the potter's wheel.
I cast you from lead, from glass
In the loamy soil of my land
Where the Olympians appeared to mortals.
I shaped you from brass
Before I built your temples of stone
Above the banks of my rivers and lakes.
In the doorways of my tribal tents
With gilded trim and mosaic windows
I was the first to sing for you a song
In my native tongue
While Europe was mumbling for centuries
The *Pater Noster* of Rome.

In the desert, I lifted
the last drops
From my pitcher to your lips
When from whirlwinds, from thirst and heat
My people were dying, my camels and my flocks.
My oak-wood iconostasis belongs to you alone

Behold
I see you again today
You circle over me
Like a kite, like a bird of prey
My God, my eternal neighbor

Circle above me
Bind me to your altars
Don't tarry
You envious God
This minute I will go
Into the deep forests
And will chop for you
Firewood in piles.
Ignite your rage!
And cast me into the fire alive
Naked the way I was born
And watch me burn
As you watched
Jan Hus the Bohemian burn

I know you will be very pleased
When in your paradise
There is the smell
Of my roasting blood

And if you do not want
To set fire to the stake
I will hand you a sword
To cut me to pieces
Like a broken toy

And if you want
Take away my name
Only teach me, teach me God
How to love without pain

SISYPHUS AND I

When I ceased to celebrate your fame
You threatened me
You would destroy
My wild game
You would destroy
The harvest of my fields

In spite of that my land is full of deer
In spite of that my vineyards
Are heavy with grapes

Don't ask me now
"To whom shall I offer my gifts
Made of redwood, of stone and light?"
Don't ask me now
"To whom shall I dedicate
My work of colors and words?"

If you will, my Lord
Extinguish my sight
I will be guided by the beat of my blood
And the armies of the blind
Towards any kingdom in the world
Let us talk face to face, my Lord
Without shackles or bars.
Hmm, you don't want to?
I see your blood red icons
Looking at me with a frown
From the Byzantine altars.

If you will
Press me down
To the cobblestones of your temples
With your leaden likeness
And hold me there

Bind my arms with irons
To the pillars.
With my teeth I will hew out
On the shores of Oregon
The craggy face
Of Abraham Lincoln

God, you created the earth
And the heavens
After your own image
You created man and woman
Tell me, Lord, is it true
That you made
The cannibals
After your likeness too?

Songs of the Mount

Translated by Donald Hitchcock

Like thirsty flocks
I let my prayers go
To look for the holy waters
In the canyons of the white river
Where my mother carried me
Before my birth

And in the manger of Byzantine structures
My first nourishment
Was served to me on sabers
By brigands and rebel chiefs

And in the church
Where I was baptized
I lifted my hands
And I spoke to the people
Not to the simple magi
Who hailed my advent among you

Since that time I stride the Earth
From sea to sea
And light a star for every newborn

Come unto me
Those whose passion has been broken
Come unto me
Those who have not yet succeeded
In killing themselves

Come unto me
You wise connoisseurs of sorrow

Come unto me
Those who are dressed in blindness
I assure you, you will see

Come unto me
You who have not yet discovered
The likeness of the sea

Come unto me
Those who have been consumed
By homesickness like my love.
On the gallows of your grief
I hung with you for centuries

Today my blond young boy and I
Will crown you with feasts
With countless springtimes of joy
Come unto me
You who have committed adultery
In your own home

Come unto me
Those who have been suffocated in
The disasters of Sodom

I will raise my hands
And there I will grow rows
Of blooming cherry trees
For your morning walk

Behold
From the burning mouth of the Lord
Naked harlots of Gomorrah are jumping
With bitten bosoms and hips
They are running into my embrace
They are rushing to my rescuing lips

Come unto me
Those who are thirsty!
I will pour waterfalls
Into your scorched throats
The radiance
Of the mountain rivers of my soul
Come unto me
Those who have turned your roads
Into hazardous games
Come unto me
Those who are in love with their chains

Come unto me
Those who have been evicted

From your farmlands
From your dreams

Come unto me
Widows, orphans, and strangers
I bequeath to you
The summer palaces of my heart

Come unto me
Those who have fallen
Deep into degradation
You know the Earth is hard

From the sound of my voice
I will mold for you wings
For your blood
For the winds

Come unto me
Beggars, no need for alms
I exhort you to sit down
At the plentiful tables of my wedding
In thousands of Moscows

Above the horizons of my brows
Raise your goblets of wine
Lift up your beautiful brides

For you I will draw
From inside my mind
Mountains of olives
And pomegranate groves

Come unto me
Those who have not yet discovered
The greatness of your lips
I will barter with you for kisses
Millions of my rainbow smiles

Come unto me
Escapees of asylums
Come unto me those
Who are expected
By Pontius Pilate
At the foot of Golgotha
Come, candidates for oval offices
Candidates for electric chairs
Come, candidates for passionate love
Candidates for executioners' scaffolds
Come, candidates for royal crowns
Candidates for arenas with lions
Come, candidates for the most beautiful name
Come, murderers with the mark of Cain
You alone will climb the ridges
Of your petrified pain

Come, suicide of future centuries
Leaning on the railings of bridges
Come unto me
Those who are not loved by anyone
I shall let the streams
Of my heavens flow
Through the deserts of your souls

Come unto me
You self-despisers
Seekers of your gallows, of your end
Listen to the voice
The Earth is calling my name
Ilja, you are my friend
Come unto me
Those who have been spat upon
Come unto me
Those who have been reviled
I will carry you
In the cabins of my heart
Like Noah carried
His children in the ark
Through the waters of the great flood

Come unto me
Those who have been gnawed
By icebergs of solitude
The suns of my embraces
Will ripen the grapes
Of your exiled blood

Come unto me
Banished great spirits of the red skins
My long nose is like yours
Will there be no Sun Dance
Around and around you?
Great spirit—Gitchie Manitou—

Reclaim your scattered arrows
Reclaim your quiver

Why has the iron god
on your continent
Constructed nimbuses?
You were still, you were silent
When foreign ships
Were carrying on board
A cast iron cross
For the crucifixion of your land
You were still, you were silent
When you heard next to your shores
The damned *Dominus Vobiscum*
Your red-skinned gods
Were silent
The ocean was mute
The horses said nothing

I am a juggler
From the millennium circus
Merchants of Farin were waiting for me
At the crossroads

Behold
My pupils destroyed the church
Of the Potsdam Garrison
Today, I will lift the prairie
On the horns of a bison
And the bison's voice will roar

Above the blood of dead tribes
I will set
The grief of the centuries
On my tough crown.
Look at the coast
The sea is spewing up
Pieces of my old names

In the mountains
In the passes
On the body of my love
I'll write God's
Testament in kisses
And like King David
Will cry out, Judea
And commence a song
About the eternity of people

Come unto me, good Christians
From the TV services to God on Sundays
Today I will read to you in Russian
The red posters of Jack Hirschman
Student girls with crucifixes
Student girls without
The homework for tomorrow
Kiss the feet of Christ
Christ has risen
Christ has risen
Christ has risen by kisses

In the black churches of St. Louis
Voices wailed
Glory, Glory Hallelujah!
What's the good of Hallelujah
Without a sweet kiss?
In the black churches of St. Louis
A last kiss hanged itself Last night

Come unto me, Jesus
I cry out in convulsive pain
Do you remember you said
"Let the children come unto me"?
Everyone fell silent and let them come
Then the crowd began to roar from all sides:
"You are an evildoer!"
Behold
Today on the streets of San Francisco
Lorenzo Ferlingetti is selling magazines
With details of children's suicides

Moor Jesus to my Mount
Listen to my songs
Leave the army of angels
Come unto me
Without gold, without precious stones
Only then will I know
If you, your father and mother
Are right or wrong

Come unto me
Without holy sacraments and labels
Come, you are dressed well enough

I will prepare a dinner for you
And for eternity
On my stone tables

Come unto me, Jesus
You remember
The crowd did not want Barabbas
The crowd wanted you on the cross
Then your rocket flew off into space
Then thousands of years
Among the bodiless
Then thousands of years
Of doing nothing

Abandon, Jesus, the ceremonies in heaven
You are the shepherd.
Blow your horns!
Is it not true that it is boring
To live in paradise
Without your cut nails
Without your crown of thorns?
You are needed where suffering is
And suffering here on Earth is everywhere

Come unto me, Jesus
In God we trust
So you understand, my friend
Without a cross and crucifixion
There is no Christ
Come unto me

Those who have known
For thousands of years
What belongs to Caesar
What belongs to God
Flying veils I will embroider
For your Broadway beauties
From the shreds of my mood

Come unto me, cheerful crowds
I can still hear your applause
I can still hear you shouting at me
"You are the loser!"
And I roared on the plateaus of my heart
Like a wounded Appaloosa
Come unto me
Those who have been mute
Behind your iron gates
When my solitary step
Was devouring
The wavy nights of the boulevards

I am the one who lost paradise
Without serpent, without tasty fruits
I alone drove out of heaven
Myself, my children, and my love
Then from grief, from pain
I tore my clothing
Without any judgment from above
Then I stood silent for a long time

Like a statue of bronze in a Baroque garden
And through the forgotten island of my soul
I wander today like a hungry albatross

Hey, Fisherman
The fishing gig is busted
We hug the islands by bridges
Bridges of gold
Cast iron bridges
Bridges on top of bridges
Bridges over sailboats
And under them
Bridges above the houses
And beneath them
Bridges over the seas
Bridges under the seas
Bridges over the Earth
Bridges under the Earth
Everyone to his place
Stride over the bridges
Pig-iron nations

Ah, poor little Moses
The waters divide before us
And turn into dry land
Even without your magic wand
Bridges for cities without faces
Bridges for lovers
Bridges for suicides
Bridges for fishermen

Bridges for the homeless
And the whores
Bridges and under them bays
Bridges and under them
Mountains of anguish

Come unto me
Gilded miniature faces,
Masters of Babylon
Today on New York's Forty-Second Street
You are given lessons in erotica
By the mistresses of King Solomon

Come unto me, lovers of narcotics
Come unto me
Offspring of feathered warriors
Come, vagabonds and vagrants
Lying under the almond trees
Of California's harvested vineyards
I will offer you roasted wild game
From the sacrificial altars of my pagan gods
Come, Hari Krishna missionaries
Come, alcoholic millionaires' wives
Don't believe the stories
About the eye of the needle
The camel and heaven
I will find for you a wonderful retreat
Under the fig trees

I know after your whiskey
You will love my meals
You will love my meat

Push away the guards of your slack bodies
I know you fear me
Like the Romans feared the armies of Hannibal
I don't need a cavalry or elephants
Behold, the great river Amazon
Each morning offers refreshments
To every cannibal

Come unto me, sinners of Manhattan
Come in jeans, come in cassocks
Come, go-go girls
Topless and bottomless
In the nightclubs of New Orleans
I can hear the beat of your heavy breasts
I can hear your drums
The Lord sees you
Verily I say
He will rush to smell the aroma
Under your arms

Come, prostitutes in your shaggy sackcloths
Come children, come criminals
Come, little girls
You have been raped under the Brooklyn Bridge
Come unto me
You who were deceived in paradise

Come, Eves without fig leaves
Come with hidden nakedness
Come without clothing
I will awaken your hopes
I will tell the meaning of your dreams
I will dress you today
In the rainbow of spring
Destroy the coat hangers of your souls.

With the waters of thousands of Niagara Falls
I will wash away your sins
I will open for you
The road to heaven

Only one thing I ask of you
When you approach the gates of Eden:
Please read my verses to the Lord

Sisyphus and I

Translated by Jack Hirschman

Sisyphus told the river god Asopus that his daughter Aegina had been abducted by Zeus. Sisyphus was punished for telling the secret by being condemned eternally to roll an enormous stone up the slope of a mountain. Each time it nearly reached the summit, it only rolled down again.

In the Black Hills of the Dakotas
Stone masons hammer into my face
I am the one who rolled the stones
Onto the banks of the Chesapeake Bay

No oxen pulled my stones
I had no Egyptian slaves like the pharaohs
No builders like in Greece, like in Rome

From quarries I stole stones
Tore them out by the roots
My hands stone-hard
My muscles stone-hard
Like Robinson Jeffers in Carmel
I wanted to build stairs of stones
To the skies
And down to the seas
Come, gods, one by one
Behold us and compare

SISYPHUS AND I

Sisyphus the demigod and me
I was born next to your land
They called me the barbarian
Did I steal any secrets
From your sacred shrine?
Did I curse you by my pagan idols?
Did I scorn you?
Did I condemn your holy mind?
Behold the stones, they are not mine
Behold my altars without sacrificial horns

Tell me, gods, which one of you
Bound me to the cliffs?
Why did you place me among the thieves?

Not just the one stone
In the myth of Sisyphus
But thousands of stones
Came pouring down on me
Stones came rolling over me
They whistled above me
They crashed into the sea
I pushed them again and again
And they would fall down
And I would push them again
I do not understand
Why I kept pushing them up
Again and again and again
Up to the top of the hill

And they would fall down
And I would push them again
I do not understand
Why I kept pushing them up
Again and again and again

What did I want?
What end did I desire?
To what Zeus, what Cronos, what Baal
Did I bring sacrifices
On my craggy heights?

What beauty did I worship?
Tired and dispirited
I did not know.
I wept, I roared
And thousands of times
I stained the stones with my blood
Like Christ his cross
Sisyphus, Sisyphus
Did you hear my call?
Our common fate is to push stones
You—only one, and I—thousands

Sisyphus is silent
Zeus and Cronos are silent
The tormented prisoners are silent
On the islands
Of Aistates and Makronisos

And I am silent too
And I still do not understand
Why I push my stones up
Again and again and again

The Song of My Love

Translated by Jack Hirschman

For millions of years
The earth played
With the waters of the great seas
Then my Love was born
The wild sunflowers open up
In the mornings
When they see my Love
Walking on the prairies
The body of my Love
Is a shapely royal palm
On the avenues
Of the southern shores
Behold the wonder of wonders
Inhabitants of the Earth
And the heavens
Seekers of the road to El Dorado
In the fast-flowing waters
Of Colorado
My beloved refreshes her beautiful legs
Tanned by the sun of Arizona
The eyes of my Love
Are the mountain lakes of Sierra Laguna
At the sources of the Rio Grande.

From the azure lakes of my Love
The Apaches speak to their god
The movements of my Love's arms
Are the dancing fountains
In the palaces
Of the old city of Prague
The lashes of my Love
Are the lilies beneath the cypress
In the waters of the Everglades
The hair of my love is like the vineyards
On the slopes of Ohrid and Struga
I am the harvester of the sweetness of her grapes
At times of struggle
In the abyss of my heart
My Love is the first olive tree
Of Mount Ararat
The step of my Love
Is the light step of antelopes
On the wave-like hills of Montana
The lips of my Love
Are the sunrises and sunsets
Between two oceans
The words of my Beloved
Are the fields
Of the land of Canaan
Where the milk and honey flow
When my Love sings
Her voice is like a polyphony
Of mountains and seas
The kisses of my Love
Are the blooming orange groves
In the valleys of California

The spirit of my Beloved
Is the wind drenched in springtime
On the summits of Mount Pirin
When I look at my Love
My heart rejoices
As the ancient Persian tribes
Rejoiced during the feast of Purim
When my Love leaves me
My longing plays with my grief
Like the Caribbean hurricane
Plays with the sea
My Love is a spring in the desert
Where the thirsting
Caravan of my soul
Hastens to drink its fill

Sermon at the Washington Monument

Translated by Donald Hitchcock

The Beatnik poet Ferlinghetti
Told me once
The Anglo-Saxons speak the truth
With half-closed mouths
With half-closed mouths it is easy to lie
That's why I will lift up my voice today
And speak to you

Poets of the Capitol of the United States
Poets from Georgetown, Poets from Chevy Chase
Your heavy faces resemble lobsters and steaks

Get out from your well-heated lavatories
From behind your facades, your rusted chariots
Look at the sky—heaven is pregnant
Very soon it will give birth to some
New rhyme of free-versed idiots
I hear America is not singing anymore
All songs are dead
And you are the executioner
I hear the bums, the hungry, the abused
I hear the city with Japanese cherry trees
Victorian homes and decorated girls

I hear drunkards at midnight, at noon
I hear people who have walked on the moon
I hear museums with spaceships and Cherokee bones
I hear the monuments to assassinated presidents
I hear the tears without pillows
I hear the ghosts of thousands of haunted houses
I hear the homes with eternal agonies
I hear Pentagons
I hear the first lady singing with Sinatra
To benefit the crippled and the poor
I hear tycoons, I hear the homeless
I hear the fireworks on the Fourth of July
I hear the filibusters
I hear the religious crusaders
I hear the public and the hidden bastards
I hear gurus and God Bless America
I hear the police in bulletproof vests
Shooting and being shot
I hear newspaper boys
I hear acrobats, politicians, diplomats
I hear rock fans and Redskins fans
I hear the moral majority
I hear criminal killers, victims, soul healers
I hear the lesbians and the gays
I hear the internal radiance of the street
I hear Jehovah's Witnesses
I hear readers of the Wall Street Journal
I hear the city's springs and winters
I hear the money printers
I hear drug dealers, crime dealers

I hear dealers in dreams
I hear dealers in God
I hear dealers in beauty
I hear dealers in foreign kings
I hear dealers in kids and guns
Dealers in houses and justice
I hear dealers in insanity, in dictators
Law dealers, playboy dealers, body dealers
Dealers in theocracy
Dealers in liberty and democracy
I hear the mighty plutocracy

Only you are silent,
Poets of the Capitol of the United States of America.
There were times when mighty kings and czars feared poets
Thousands of years ago the youth gathered
To listen to Ovid the singer of Rome
He was driven for his songs out of his home
By Augustus the Emperor
Have you ever known François Villon
Who multiplied his life on the gallows?
Have you ever known Lord Byron
Who died for the liberty of the Hellens?

Who fears your songs?
Who fears your chirping?
Do they whisper your lines
Those who are in love?
Do they seek comfort in your words
Those who are in despair?

Who wants to wear the rags of your spirit?
Who wants to breathe the pollution of your mind?
I know your only worry is
Whether your daughters made progress in ballet courses
Or riding Arabian horses
I would rather go to the southeast corners of this city
And listen to the tales of the toothless and the drunk

Why do you dye the gray hair of your souls?
Behold, the road to the heart lies only through the heart
You are the bad players in the game of art
Come from your beaten paths, come from your private roads

I, Ilja Kostovski, multilingual bard
Teacher, philosopher, and tireless wanderer
Will stride your Bethesda streets
In the dress of a medieval rat catcher
And will sing for you Apollinaire's *Alcohols*
With the ozone of my songs
I will crush your hundred-story boredom

Did you hear Zarathustra
Exhorting you to break the windows
And go into the fresh air?

Oh no, you wimps never broke a window in your lives
You have fancy fences and alarm systems
You have plenty of food for your wives, for your dogs
But your songs are malnourished

You are nameless and voiceless
Without identity, without a piece of eternity
To whom will you offer your pages?

My words will never die
I dug for them in the mountains of time
My cry will be carved in the stone of ages
I, Ilja Kostovski the stuntman
Want to show you today
My daring jumps off racehorses
Under the ruined pillars of the Reichstag
From the copper roofs where the Russian soldiers
Raised the red flag
I will bring you ash
From the barbecued flesh of millions

Behold!
Today the President of the United States
On Pennsylvania Avenue
Will preach a sermon on how to survive a nuclear war
Behold, worn-out prophets
I know you scorn my word-sabers
Today I will give you roles
To act in my puppet plays

I will hem the futures of your sons
With the broken pieces of dreams and kisses
I have gathered in the Anacostia slums

AFTERWORD

Gallows Praise

A Glance into Ilja Kostovski's Selected Poetry

David Keplinger

It is a slightly smirking smile that accompanies the voice calling on Muses in Ilja Kostovski's epic poetry and final book, *Sisiphus and I.* In this seminal production of the poet's work, an eager, if slightly sarcastic, voice cries out from the woodpile of modernity:

Don't tarry
You envious God
This minute I will go
Into the deep forests
And will chop for you
Firewood in piles.

As for Kostovski's readers, they are the "connoisseurs of sorrow," the "suicides…leaning on the railings of bridges," the "self-despisers," for he is a poet of the lone wolves, the melancholy wanderer we read about in Blake and imagine among the happy crowds at Coney Island in the 1920s, or among the tripping multitudes of Haight Ashbury in the 1960s, or in the city where he made his last residence, the throngs of the upright and enraged of Washington, D.C.

Kostovski's verse is prayer to a God who is or is not there, a nearly desperate, repeating "Come unto me." It is not merely exhortation to the deity. He invokes, too, the gathering crowds of the lost and broken-hearted, as though the divine could only be conjured by those numbers, or as if the dead God of Nietzsche could be resurrected by a hoard whose suffering is the very thing that binds them. In that case, instead of a savior, the hero of these poems is a common wound: "Come unto me those/Who have turned your roads/Into hazardous games." The language is straight out of the book of Micah (whose own anaphoric language begins each chapter with "Hear"), an Old Testament prophet no one believes, but the language pops with contemporary hideousness: "Come, candidates for oval offices/ Come, candidates for electric chairs."

In what is perhaps the most powerful poem in the collection, "Sermon at the Washington Monument," Kostovski the poet recalls his association with Ferlinghetti, who "Told me once/The Anglo-Saxons speak the truth/ with half-closed mouths..." From a formal angle, the collection *Sisyphus and I* is Kostovski's open-mouthed song to a universe that may or may not be listening. Like the fledgling with mouth turned upward, Kostovski's poetry is both artistic hallelujah and hungry yawp, whose overarching tone is a kind of "gallows praise": "I hear America is not singing anymore/All songs are dead/And you are the executioner.../Have you ever known Francois Villion/ Who multiplied his life on the gallows?" The poet calls on writers to awaken—rather like Micah, standing on his street corner—if not to save anything, then to attend it as it passes, flares out, at the height of its beauty.

Kostovski, born in the Macedonian province of Greece, is the author of *Dostoevsky and Goethe: Two Devils, Two Geniuses*. Like his poetry, his scholarship sought out the insight of the outsider, as he himself carried the burden of his generation through exile during Communist overthrows, until he settled in Washington, D.C. The prophetic insight is this: a monument does not memorialize a country, but rather a misinterpreted ideal. The best remembrances are those that serve a human purpose. And the best invitation to the gods, in Kostovski's reckoning at least, is to chop some firewood, good for burning. This is a poet whose voice at once harkens back to the *Tanakh* while it recalls the beatniks of San Francisco, the homeless, and the insidious white power structures and silent mausoleums of Washington D.C. We are reminded in these pages that life is to be sung open-mouthed, if at all.

David Keplinger
December, 2017

Ilja Kostovski was a Macedonian poet and literary scholar. A refugee from the Greek Civil War, he was illiterate at the age of 14 but managed to receive his PhD in Comparative Literature at Prague's Charles University by the age of 32. He taught Russian literature and languages at universities in Prague, Berlin, Potsdam, and Heidleberg. He also taught at the University of Maryland and the College of William and Mary. He is the author of the scholarly work *Dostoyevski and Goethe: Two Devils, Two Geniuses. Sisyphus and I* is Kostovski's first and only collection of poems. He lived in the Washington, DC area for over 40 years until his death in 2017.

Jack Hirschman is an American poet, writer, literary translator, essayist, and social activist. He received his Ph.D. at Indiana University and he has published over 50 books of poetry, including A *Correspondence of Americans* (1960), *The Arcanes* (2006), and *All That Is Left* (2008). In 2012, he became Poet Laureate of San Francisco, the first person ever to be given this honor. He lives and creates in San Francisco.

Donald Hitchcock received his Ph.D. at Harvard University and taught Russian Literature and Old Church Slavonic at the University of Maryland for over 40 years, until his death in 2017.

Jordan Plevneš was born in 1953 in Macedonia. He writes plays, novels, poetry, and essays. His works have been translated into over 50 languages. Since 1988 he has lived in Paris, where he taught creative writing and was Ambassador of the Republic of Macedonia to France, Spain, Portugal, and UNESCO. Since 2007, he has been president of the University of Audiovisual Arts, European Film Academy (ESRA), Paris-Skopje-New York.

David Keplinger is the author of five collections of poetry, most recently *Another City* (Milkweed, 2018), *The Most Natural Thing* (New Issues, 2013) and *The Prayers of Others* (New Issues, 2006), which won the Colorado Book Award. Keplinger has been awarded a two-year Soros Foundation fellowship and two fellowships by the National Endowment for the Arts. His translations of Danish poet Carsten René Nielsen have appeared in two volumes, *World Cut Out with Crooked Scissors* (2007) and *House Inspections* (2011), a Lannan Translations Selection; and his collaboration with German poet Jan Wagner, titled *The Art of Topiary*, was published in 2017 by Milkweed Editions. He directs the Master of Fine Arts program in Creative Writing at American University in Washington, DC.

www.ingramcontent.com/pod-product-compliance
Lightning Source LLC
LaVergne TN
LVHW051021080826
845145LV00009B/2732